The French De

A Pompey Fan's Disastrous Trip To The Euro

Lee Freeman

To some of the Pompey family

Oily, Routhy, Guesty, Suzy, Westwood, Popham, Roger Beale, Sammy Seagull, Walshie, Gary, Linda, Steve, Harvey, Mutant, Simon, Tom, Nick, Brad, Olly, Loz, Stefan the Swede, Leffe, Fisher, Mark, Jax, Samantha, Richard, Tina & Dave.

Shant on!

Chapters

Introduction 4

Introduction

As I stood in the away end of Plymouth Argyle's Home Park I watched as the Argyle supporters erupted into raptures as Plymouth celebrated scoring an injury time winner to send my team Portsmouth crashing out of the playoffs. It meant confining us to another season of having to endure watching league two football and putting up with the shockingly terrible standard of league two referees. Being a Pompey fan since the mid 1980's I'm used to my fair share of disappointments and conceding so late into injury time was not a shock but more expected and sure enough it arrived right on it's stoppage time cue. As the ball was headed home it was more of a case of "and there it is" from Pompey fans as opposed to being shocked and devastated that we had blown it so late on in a game. This was Pompey after all and a team that had managed to throw enough points away in injury time over the course of the season to cost them automatic promotion. As I walked back to John Westwood's smelly mini bus I started to think about the Euros to take my mind off the latest Pompey pain I was being made to endure again. I was going to be jetting off to France in June to watch England and see if they could salvage my season after Pompey's latest failure to get out of a truly mediocre league two. I came to the conclusion that England also being perennial underachievers and banking on the theory of the law of averages would at some stage turn up at a competition and actually do something.

Hope And No Glory

As a 10 year old kid the first World Cup I ever watched was Mexico 86, which typified everything about watching England. From starting the group stages with a 1-0 defeat to then minnows Portugal followed by a dismal 0-0 draw with the might of Morocco. The only things of any note in that game was that Bryan Robson's tournament was over through injury and Ray Wilkins getting a straight red for throwing the ball at the ref. If I remember rightly that was the most accuracy poor old 'Butch' managed in the game. Then England beat both Poland, and Paraguay 3-0 to once more build the hopes up of the nation. After those two victories we faced Argentina and I experienced my first of England's many heroic failures. I remember feeling rage and devastation as Steve Hodge's crap back pass to a despairing Peter Shilton who's feet seemed to be nailed to the ground allowing Diego Maradona to punch Argentina into the lead leaving me on the brink of tears and with genuine concerns on how I could carry on with life if England got knocked out of the quarter finals. Then a few minutes later I watched with a mixture of disbelief and despair as Maradona burst into high speed and waltzed past half the England team, including Peter Reid and Terry Fenwick as they frantically jogged after him as fast as they could. More to the point what were Fenwick and Reid even doing at a World Cup anyway? So after feeling rightly robbed in '86 it was on to Euro '88 in Germany and my first European Championships. I remember watching an interview with Glenn Hoddle who said he believed that England would taste glory and win the competition. I thought that if a player like Hoddle was saying that then England must be certain to win it. The only things it was memorable for was England losing the opening game to the Republic of Ireland and watching Marco Van Basten hammer a hatrick past England as they capitulated. Then getting another hiding this time by the Soviet Union losing all three group games and England were well and truly home before their postcards had arrived. Italia 90, Euro 96, France 98, Euro 2004 stand out as the heroic failures, missed penalties and terrible refereeing and a lot of heartache for myself and every other England fan. Euro 92, USA 94 qualifying, Euro 2000, Euro 2008 qualifying, Brazil 2014 were the ones that stand out in my mind as disastrous and humiliatingly bad performances by the national team over the years. I think it was probably after the defeat on penalties against Portugal in the 2006 World Cup quarter final that I realised that even with great players England are still crap. So from then on I accepted that this is what you will get from any

England team. Nations like Germany even when crap will still reach a final and usually win it. A decent Germany team will almost certainly reach a final and win it. A crap England team will be crap and get knocked straight out quicker than Audley Harrison. Everyone in the aftermath will shout out "back to grass roots," and "we need an English manager," no wait "we need a foreign manager" again. A good or even excellent England team apart from the seemingly less common heroic failures these days are more than likely to still be crap and get knocked out.

It hadn't even crossed my mind to go to the Euros in France for a second. It was only because I was reading my timeline on Facebook that I saw a post from friend and Pompey fan Nick Murphy. He said that a few of the lads were going to France for the week to watch England play Russia and Wales and that there were a couple of spaces left. With the same level of impulse decision making as Homer Simpson I messaged Nick and said I definitely wanted to go. The plan was to spend four nights in Marseille then get the train up to Lille to hopefully watch the Wales game, spend three nights there, then head back to England via Calais and a ferry crossing. Melissa, the wife of Tom Lodge who was also going to the Euros organised everything including flights and accommodation. Simon 'Simples' Milne who looks a lot like Gareth Southgate but without looking like a horse was going as well. Simples is totally insane when it comes to Pompey and watching football.

Not only does he watch Pompey home and away which includes pre season

friendly tours abroad he also watches non league games locally and does a fair

amount of England games including going to previous Euros. Brad and Jay were

the other two who were coming as well. I didn't really know them, but they are

faces you recognise at away games. The other person definitely going was Haydn

Hollis a defender for Notts County and a Pompey fan who goes to the Pompey

games whenever he can. I'd only met him once before and that was in the

Newcome Arms pub before the first leg of the playoff semi final against Plymouth

in May. Really nice, friendly lad, and watched him play at Fratton Park earlier in

the season. Notts County had been terrible that day and got hammered 4-0 but I

have to say that he was easily their best player by a country mile. Haydn's mum

Ange is a big Pompey fan and travels down from the Midlands to watch Pompey

whenever she can as well as going to a lot of away games. One particular game

back in the Premier league days Pompey were playing Chelsea at Stamford Bridge

when Frank Lampard went over to take a corner where the Pompey fans were sat.

As Lampard walked over to the corner flag Ange decided to flash her tits at him!

Lampard got full view of them, laughing his head you see him looking over pointing. If you go on YouTube and type in 'Lampard having a laugh with Pompey fans' you can watch it. So everytime Haydn Hollis touched the ball half the Fratton End sang "Haydn Hollis, we've seen your mum's tits!" Fair play to him though his team had just got thumped 4-0, thousands of Pompey fans for most of the game sang about seeing his mum's tits and he still came over and applauded the piss taking Pompey fans at the end. He was going to go straight to Lille for the Wales game as that was the earliest he could get out to France as he was on holiday when the rest of us were going to be flying out.

It meant that I had to join the England supporters club in order to get a ticket for the Euros. It cost me about 70 quid and only lasted for two tournaments, and France 2016 being the last one it was already close to expiring, what a rip off still charging me full me price! I had to apply for the Russia and Wales tickets through the FA for a chance to get them officially. I only managed to get a ticket for the Russia game but was more than happy with that. England had only been allocated 5000 official tickets for the Wales game so the likelihood of getting a Wales ticket was remote to say the least. I wasn't bothered about missing out on the Wales game as there were going to be fanzones around and I was looking forward to going to some of them. To me the thought of just being out in France at the Euros having a good time was good enough for me.

A lot of people I spoke to said that they wished they were going and that I was going to have a great time out there. I was looking forward to it but I kind of just forgot all about it for a while. It had been arranged and booked in December so there was plenty of other things that were going on for me up until June. Before the Euros I got to live out a childhood dream of playing a match at Fratton Park. It was superbly organised by Pompey in the community, and worth every penny of the £125 it cost me to live the Pompey dream for the evening. For my money I got a brief tour of the ground, a kit with my name and number on it. So I got to be a 'full kit wanker' and get away with it! We had Pre match warm up routines the same as the players do which was really great although there were a few of the players blowing out their arses during it. Walking into the changing rooms at Fratton Park and seeing a shirt with my name and number on it hung up waiting for me was a sight for sore eyes. Coming out of the tunnel on to the pitch and playing 90 minutes at Fratton Park on the hallowed turf while wearing Pompey colours really was a dream come true for me. It was an amazing and unforgettable night although I did manage to injure my left knee after going up for a header. I landed on it with full force and to my surprise the Fratton pitch was actually really dry and very hard. I knew straight away I'd damaged it, but I was never going to come off in a million years so I just played on through the pain, not quite Terry Butcher for England all those years ago! The following day I went to get out of bed, tried to take a step and ended up taking a dive head first landing face down on the bedroom floor. I was as stiff as a board from the game but my knee had totally locked after injuring it during the match. It was a real struggle just trying to go up and down the stairs for the next few days and it only seemed to get slightly better in that time. After a week of hobbling around I limped myself to the hospital where the doctor told me that I had badly bruised my knee and damaged some tendons, but no ligament damage. I was happy that it was just that and nothing more serious as having an injured knee in France would literally have been a pain.

In the March I took my oldest son to watch the friendly at Wembley between England and Holland. I thought I might get a bit more motivated about watching England if I was taking a game in before the Euros. England friendlies have always been a struggle to sit through especially home games at Wembley. The weather was horrendous and rained non stop all day and all night so much so that we both got soaked to the skin. The game was really boring and the ground was full of plastic Premier League fans which is just not my thing. The atmosphere was non existent and after about 10 minutes I'd had enough of it and was wondering what the earliest time I could leave without it being a total write off would be. The highlight for me was giving the Southampton players a "good scumming" (shouting "Scummer, Scummer" over and over) every time one of their players or former players touched the ball. Watching an England friendly live is actually more painful than watching it on TV which after having to endure ITV's coverage of England friendlies I didn't think would be possible. The game was so dull we both decided it was time for a fire drill and headed to the exits with about 20 minutes to go.

Going to the Holland friendly certainly didn't motivate me to go to anymore non competitive England games for the foreseeable future. I wasn't that upset as usually when it gets close to the start of a tournament everything clicks into gear and the excitement starts to build. I don't think it was until about a week before I was due to leave for France that my excitement finally started to build. I watched a really good documentary about the England team from Euro 96 with Alan Shearer going around interviewing England players, Skinner and Baddiel. It really did flick a switch in me after watching that documentary especially after Gazza said he didn't reach that cross against Germany in the semi final as he thought that the keeper would have got a touch on it that would have meant knocking it into Gazza's path for a match winning tap in. I remembered back to those fine margins that went against England that night and suddenly it felt like it had just happened yesterday and not twenty years ago.

The following morning I woke up buzzing with anticipation of the upcoming Euros and with thoughts of wanting to knock Gareth Southgate out all over again. Wanting to chin Southgate aside I was excited about the Euros and set off in my car to work when I decided to have a blast of Three Lions on my stereo. It sounded brilliant! I hadn't listened to it for years but suddenly 20 years on and with my first trip to a competition watching England it really did add to my excitement. The last time I had felt like that was Euro 96 which really was a special time, not just with the England team Britpop was everywhere, Oasis ruled the world and Only Fools and Horses made a brief comeback. So for the rest of the week my journey to and from work was listening to a mixture of Britpop, Skinner, Baddiel and the Lightning Seeds! Working in sales for a financial services company the main part of the job is to make as many sales as possible and one of the best ways of doing that is to have great rapport with your customers. That's a part of the job I've always been really good at. As the Euros drew closer I'd often have a brief conversation with my customers and tell them that I was off to watch England play in France. Whatever I was saying must have worked as my sales shot up over that period before I went off to the Euros. One of my customers was former Millwall and Pompey goalkeeper Brian Horne. I recognised the name when I first spoke to him, but it wasn't until he said he used to be a footballer that I realised who he was. He was a really nice guy, proper London boy an I ended up having a good chat with him about playing for Millwall and his time with Pompey. I love getting the inside info on my team from ex players or someone who works at the club. That kind of gossip is like gold dust when you're having a few beers down the pub before a game. I told him I was off to the Euros but didn't have tickets for the Wales game and that they were pretty scarce. He told me he had a few tickets for some games including the Wales one and wanted to sell them. I said I'd message the lads and see if they wanted them and let him know. The price for the Wales tickets were more expensive than my Pompey season ticket, which I could never justify paying out for. Simples and Jay already had tickets for the

Wales game, I think Jay paid close to £400 for the ticket but nobody else wanted to pay anywhere near that much for a ticket.

It got closer to finally going and I decided that I wanted to take a George Cross flag with me that had something about Pompey on it. Unfortunately I left it too late to get one made so had to go with the only one I had at home which was bought for my kids at the Pompey shop a couple of years back. I wanted one with the new badge on it but the Pompey shop is just a Sports Direct shop which basically sells their mass produced crap plus Pompey kits. There was no chance of getting a new flag from there so I went with the flag I already had. The important thing was that it had Portsmouth on it.

The day before I was due to leave I went out on my lunch break from work and impulse bought a red England shirt for the trip. I've always preferred England wearing red to white, maybe it's because we won the World Cup in 1966 wearing red I don't know. So with a day to spare I had everything ready for the trip laid out on the bed. I took a picture of it and posted it on Facebook including the Pompey Fans page. I got a lot of messages from other Pompey fans asking me to have a safe trip and to post plenty of pictures of my time at the Euros on.

As the morning of the departure from England arrived I was ready to go and was really excited to actually be going to a major tournament to watch England. I'm one of those people who tries to do and see as many things in life as possible and going to the Euros was definitely a good one to have on the must do list. As always when I woke up I picked up my tablet and read the news. My heart sank when I read the main headline. It said "and so it begins." Then I saw the pictures and read the article. It said that England fans had been rioting and singing songs about ISIS asking where they were and there's pork on the barbecue. I didn't really think about there being trouble at the Euros I thought that those days were in the past. I did also read that Marseille Ultras had been involved in the trouble as well. I hoped that by the time we had landed the police would have been able to show their presence and that would be the end of that.

I took the train from Fratton station and headed to Heathrow via a bus from Woking. The journey didn't drag and I was at the airport in no time. I met up with all the guys, shook their hands and said hello. We didn't hang around as we

17

wanted to get checked straight in so we could head to the bar and get the trip started. As we looked for the Wetherspoons we noticed we were being followed by half a dozen police officers.

When I realised that we were being followed, I slowed down so they could catch up with me. When they did I made a joke to one of them that we hadn't had chance to do anything wrong yet. One of the coppers asked me if we were all Pompey fans. I was surprised how he knew who we supported, so I asked the copper how he could tell that we were all Pompey fans. He joked "well all of your mates have Pompey tattoos which gives it away!" I thought 'funny fucker!' So I asked him if he could spot where the airport Wetherspoons was! To be fair he did point the way to where the Wetherspoons was and wished us a safe trip. It was great to get to the bar albeit the Heathrow airport bar and finally get a few overpriced rounds in. For some reason Simples was happy for us to pay £6 for a Jaeger bomb for him when we were getting the drinks in. I swear he dodged getting a round in at Heathrow! There were quite a few Wales fans there in the bar as well who were stood with us and it was a good fun having a bit of banter with them. They were Cardiff fans and knew we were all Pompey fans and started chatting to us. Back in the hooligan days of the 1980's Pompey and Cardiff had a fair bit of rivalry with each other. Cardiff fans pulled down the Pompey clock in the Milton End at Fratton Park, with the clock supposedly ending up back in Wales. In turn the Pompey 6:57 crew travelled up to Cardiff wearing suits and having had fake wedding invitations made to fool the police that they were actually going to a real wedding meaning that they could have a dust up with the Cardiff firm. A bit before my time but that story is part of Pompey folklore.

Our first flight was to Madrid as we had to change before we could get to Marseille. We only had a short stop at Madrid airport so we all went to check in and wait in the departure area. Somehow Jay lost his boarding pass and had to go and buy another one which cost him I think about 40 Euros. Food wise there wasn't really a great deal to choose from so we ended up having to get something from McDonalds. We found a bar right by the departure lounge and had a beer while we waited to board the plane. As people started making their way to the plane we finished our beers and headed over to queue up to get on the plane to take us to Marseille. The plane was only a tiny one, certainly the smallest I'd ever been on. I noticed that the entire plane was full of just England fans. I think there was one woman who was a passenger the rest were guys who by now had certainly had had more than a few drinks.

It was without doubt the funniest flight I've ever been on. It was like being on

a massive stag do but with just England fans. Everyone was getting excited and a

bit more rowdy as we were getting closer to landing and starting our respective

trips. There were a couple of hostesses on the flight and one of them just so

happened to be really pretty and of course every guy on board soon realised this

before we had even taken off. There was a button located just above everyones'

head which you could press to call the stewardess over if you needed anything. Of

course once one of the guys pressed it and she came over to them, then the next

one did it. Each time she walked over to a passenger she bent over with dozens of

guys killing themselves laughing. The stewardess soon caught on that most of the

plane was trying to get her to bend over for them. She then stood at the front of

the plane and had a go at everyone for pressing the buttons and said that it was

only to be pressed if anybody actually wanted her help. The stewardess then went

to go and get the drinks ready but didn't come back as half the men on the flight

were all frantically pressing the buttons in order to get her attention. All you

could hear was 'bing ,bing, bing' and blue lights coming on up and down the plane.

It was hilarious as I watched all of these hands sticking up pressing buttons at the

same time as each other. Watching all of these blue lights going on and off, I thought to myself 'yeah, she won't be serving drinks to anyone!' Sure enough no one got served a drink on the entire flight. Just after the button pushing frenzy had finally stopped an England fan run down the aisle and picked up the receiver for the personal address system. He then started singing "Eng-er-land, Eng-er-Land," everyone was in fits of laughter and then joined in singing. I wouldn't have been surprised if the stewardess hadn't locked herself in the cockpit for the rest of the journey. For some strange reason our flight landed 20 minutes early in Marseille. I'm going to take a stab in the dark and guess that the pilots plus stewardesses were so pissed off with us they just wanted to get shot of the England fans-come-lads-stag-do as quickly as possible.

Some Like It Not

We walked straight over to the taxi rank outside of Marseille airport and grabbed a couple of taxis. Me, Tom and Simples jumped in one taxi while Nick and Brad got another one together. We could have jumped on a bus and saved some money but everyone was tired and just wanted to get checked in as soon as possible. The journey was about a 20 minute drive to the city from the airport which is located on the outskirts of Marseille. For some reason the taxi driver dropped us off by the train station and not by our hotel. As we got out the car not exactly knowing where we were, I looked around at the surroundings while taking it all in and said out loud "what a fucking shit hole!" It really was an awful place. As I stood there I could smell the stench of dried piss coming up from the pavement. There were immigrants from Africa everywhere just sat around in groups on the street not doing anything other than watching us getting out of a taxi. The street was full of rubbish, like when a fox has decided to have a go at your rubbish bag on bin day and there is crap left all over the pavement. I'd always known that Marseille was a dive, but until I was actually there I really didn't realise just how bad it was.

After quarter of an hour of the Sat Nav on my phone sending the three of us in the wrong direction we finally found the right way to the hotel. We checked in and went up to our rooms, the best way of describing the rooms was that they were tired, well more like totally shagged out in all honesty. It wasn't the greatest room and was in need of some urgent updating but it was just about acceptable for what we needed and if we did get hungry the hotel did have a vending machine to use! Who needs room service anyway when your hotel has a vending machine in the reception area? I was pretty tired after a day's travelling and already realising Marseille was the dump I feared it would be I was happy to throw the towel in and head straight to bed and get some sleep. The rest of the lads though wanted to have look around, find where the other England fans were and have a few drinks. So I thought I might as well take a wonder and see what Marseille had to offer on a Friday night apart from piss smelling pavements.

We weren't really sure where we were going and ended up leaving the main road that we were on and started walking down some side roads that didn't look the best to be walking down. The area we were in certainly wasn't somewhere you would see being advertised by the French tourist board. The further we walked down the side roads the worse it became. Marseille has a high Muslim population at around 40%, and we must have stumbled into the neighbourhood where it was 100%. As we walked through the streets we noticed that there were groups of men with beards like Bin Laden stood just staring at us. We carried on down the street going past them almost at a canter now looking like a group of English idiots who really did have no idea where they were going. We kept our heads down and looked straight on until we turned the corner. We then turned left into another small road and headed down it, still with one eye over our shoulders as we did think we were likely to start being followed. We definitely did feel like we had unwittingly ended up in a no go part of town. After walking past a couple of Mosques with even more people staring at us we finally came to the end of the road which took us to the port. We could see it was a mix of people with a lot of England fans walking around and sitting outside the various bars having a drink and enjoying the night. We made our way around the port trying to get an idea of what was in the area and see what the port of Marseille looked like at night. The port did look fairly picturesque and was certainly the nicest part of the city I'd seen so far. We strolled along the port where there had been trouble the previous night between England fans, the French police and Marseille Ultras. I could still see a lot of smashed green glass on the road and pavements as we looked at the bars that had gotten wrecked during the trouble from the previous

night. We could hear England fans singing a couple of roads away from where we

were, so we decided to head over to them and see what was happening. There

was a group of about 200 England fans stood outside a bar in the corner of the

square having a sing song and a good time. It didn't look like we were going to be

getting served anytime soon so we carried on down the square to another bar

where there were a lot less England fans who were sat outside having a drink.

These England fans were just chatting quietly and where there wasn't so many

fans we were able to get served a lot quicker than if we had tried to get a drink at

the other bar. After having a beer we walked back towards the bar where the

large group of England fans were now being watched from two different areas by

French riot police. Some of the England fans were stood on tables singing, but

that was it they weren't causing any trouble, nothing was getting damaged and

everything was in good spirits. The only things happening was fans having a few

drinks and singing the same five England songs over and over. I was walking

towards the group of England fans when I started talking to another England fan

who was coming from the opposite direction. He started chatting to me and told

me about the trouble from the previous night. He said that it was a totally unprovoked attack by the Marseille Ultras who were carrying knives on them as well. He did say that they had sought out England fans just to cause trouble with them.

The rest of the guys were stood on the fringes of the group of the England fans who were still singing away. Everyone except those singing at the bar could tell that trouble was about to start. I really could feel that it was on it's was at any moment I could just sense it. The police didn't seem to like the England fans singing and I watched them edge closer to the bar where the singing was coming from. I just knew that the police were going to attack the England fans. I looked away from the bar and saw about 15 Marseille Ultras heading towards me and the England fan I was having a chat with. I nodded to my left and he looked and saw them coming our way. He said that they were the same ones from last night and that they definitely would be carrying knives on with them. They silently walked past both of us and stood by the side of the square watching the England fans without saying anything to each other. The Marseille Ultras weren't interested in me and the other guy as they wanted to have a fight with a bigger group than just two.

The Marseille Ultras looked pretty comical in all honesty. They were all young Algerians wearing funny clothes and had really bad haircuts. I think it must have been the French equivalent to a British chav. Some of them were wearing skin tight white and blue Marseille tracksuits that looked really shit like something out of the early 90's. I called Simples over and pointed the Chavvy Algerians out to him and asked him where the others were. Tom and Nick had disappeared into the crowd with Jay and we couldn't see them at all. I said to Simples and Brad that it's going to kick off in a minute and if we hang around we will be asking for trouble. The police started walking towards the England fans from the two sides that they had been stood watching from with the sole intention of breaking up the group of England fans.

So the three of us all really hungry headed back to the hotel and looked for something to eat on the way which seemed a mission in it's self as anything that was open that was selling food looked pretty awful and nothing even looked particularly recognisable. None of us bothered to buy anything to eat, so we just went straight back to the hotel. After an hour or so Tom, Nick and Jay came back from the port with Tom nursing a black eye. We asked them what had happened and Nick said that the police attacked the England fans who were singing and then the Marseille Ultras attacked the England fans as well. Tom managed to get punched when it turned into a fight between the England fans, the French police and Marseille Ultras. Nick who was still recovering from a dislocated knee ended up having to run from Marseille Ultras who were chasing him with knives but luckily enough he managed to avoid getting stabbed. So all in all a great start to the holiday, within two hours of landing one of our group had been punched, one nearly stabbed and I was starving hungry in a city where there was nothing edible to eat.

Beer On The Waterfront

Not long after waking up on our first morning at the Euros we walked to the port to get some breakfast. I was thinking about food and the others seemed to be thinking that beer was more of a suitable breakfast. We stopped off half way down the main street where there was a tiny brasserie that was slightly set back from the road. We sat down at a table outside and ordered some beers. I used to live in Sweden so I'm used to drinking strong black coffee, and there was no way I couldn't not have my morning coffee, otherwise I'd be having a splitting headache in no time and unlikely to be in the best of moods. I ordered an expresso as well as a beer, although I really couldn't see me drinking a beer that early in the day. I'm just not someone who can wake up and start drinking beer. The rest of the guys had no such problem though and were finishing their first beers as I was still drinking my expresso. After we had all finished our drinks we carried on towards the port to find something to eat as I was starving and my soul mission in life was now to find somewhere I could get some breakfast. I spotted a restaurant opposite the marina and it seemed pretty nice so everyone sat down outside where there were already some other England fans sitting. I'm pretty fluent in both Swedish and French so It was good to get to finally use my French and order everyone's food and drinks which saved them from looking like they were all playing a game of Charades with the waitress.

I was sat at the end of the table and was talking to a couple of other England fans who were on the table next to me. They had only arrived the previous day and had a similar experience to what Nick, Tom and Jay had the previous night with the Marseille Ultras. I hadn't enjoyed anything about the trip yet, but finally getting something to eat and having a chat with a couple of other England fans things were looking up.

England fans were starting to arrive at the port and it was becoming pretty busy. We left the restaurant and headed further along the port to where there were England fans arriving in their droves. It was a sea of red and white with England flags being hung everywhere around the port.

I really liked looking at the flags and seeing what teams they were and where people had travelled from in the UK. The first thing I did was look for any Pompey flags that might be about as there will always be a fair amount of Pompey fans at England games especially at the Euros. Sure enough there were Pompey fans and flags, so we ended up standing around in our own Pompey section at the port. I was having a chat with Ben Hubbard a Pompey fan from Leigh Park who knew all the same people as me. He had me in stitches dancing around with his Pompey flag in front of a Scummers one which was hanging up next to the Pompey flags for some reason. Before I knew it the port was absolutely rammed full of England fans and it was almost standing room only as literally thousands of England fans descended on the port of Marseille. The atmosphere was brilliant, everyone was singing and jumping up and down, beer flying through the air. One England fan run up to the marina across the road and dived head first into the sea. The weather was great, really sunny and hot, there were even some Brazilian dancers and drummers who turned up and were great to watch and listening to the drums it sounded like we could have been on the beach in Rio.

Our group managed to get separated from each other, as Nick and Tom were going to get the drinks in I was off wandering around making the most of being at the Euros. If I go somewhere, literally anywhere in the world then I'll always do my best to make the most of it. The England fans were certainly making the most of being in Marseille and it really was like no other party I'd ever been to before. I was posting plenty on Facebook as a lot of my friends asked me to keep them up to date with how it was all going. There was a lot of things to post that was really funny as well with so many other things going on you couldn't take all of it in. I had been mainly talking to different fans from up and down the country which was pretty interesting and good fun. When I said I was a Pompey supporter it seemed like whichever fan I spoke to regardless of what team they supported had a soft spot for Pompey. Most conversations were the usual "what happened to you lot, one minute you were winning the FA cup now you're in league two?" The quick answer I'd say was "imagine having a credit card with a massive limit, maxing it out then trying to pay it back without the money to do so!" The long version I'd tell them about how crap the different owners of the club had been over the years and that it wasn't until the Pompey fans stepped in together and bought the club that it could actually stay in existence and start rebuilding it. The fans I spoke to always seemed impressed that the club had been taken over by the supporters and always wished Pompey the best and a swift return up the leagues. One person I was talking to was so impressed that the fans had come together to save the club and that I told him that I actually helped towards funding Pompey's new training ground.

The guy was really impressed with my contribution in helping fund Pompey's new training facilities. Alright I didn't actually get around to telling him that my contribution was paying twenty five quid for a certificate to say I owned a piece of virtual turf, but after a few beers in the hot sun of Marseille that seemed like a trivial detail to mention! I had just finished telling my story about financing the new training ground when an England fan walked past me with a full length cardboard cut out of the Queen. I had to look twice, it was hilarious, I had to take a picture and post it on Facebook, my mates back home loved seeing it. There was also a cardboard Jamie Vardy floating around as well which was brilliant as every time the England fans burst in to song with 'Vardy's on fire' you would see everyone jumping up and down, beer flying through the air and the cardboard Jamie Vardy flying around above everyone's heads in the crowd. I really was having a brilliant time and I could now see what the fuss in England away games was all about. Plenty of people had told me in the past that it's always brilliant watching England play away, especially in competitions like the World Cup and at the Euros.

One of my friends back home Mike Palmer with whom I used to work as a doorman with at the notorious navy nightclub Joanna's by Southsea seafront messaged me on one of my Facebook posts. He saw that I was having a great time in Marseille and asked me if I'd be up for going to the World Cup in Russia. I messaged back saying yes and that it was a done deal, and I was well up for going to Russia! I did feel for Mike though who is a Tottenham fan that travels from Portsmouth to White Hart Lane on a regular basis to catch the home games. He was still recovering from them having a brilliant season and still finishing below Arsenal! Arsenal who in turn had an awful season yet still finished above them. Spurs, probably the only team who can finish in a Champions League place and still be able to make their fans feel like they've just been relegated!

Port Friction

There were still thousands of England fans at the port but the England party was beginning to wind down as fans were aware of the French police's and UEFA's requests to arrive at the stadium early. The request was made due to the high level of potential terrorist attacks from ISIS and other Islamic fundamentalists who seem to think that murdering innocent people is the way to go towards showing the world just how peaceful they really are. Fans needed to get to the ground as early as possible as the security would be extremely tight and it could take a bit of time to get through it all before finally being able to get inside the stadium.

With seeing the England fans starting to thin out and take down their flags I thought I'd find Simples. I gave him a call and to my surprise he answered. I asked him where he was and he said he was by the fountain which was located by the square and was around the corner from where I was. I said I'd meet him there in within the next couple of minutes. As I started to make my way around to the square I saw loads of smashed bottles and green glass all over the road and pavement. I asked an England fan what had just happened. He said that I had literally just missed a big fight and England fans were having bottles thrown at them. Because of the previous night with the Algerians in skin tight Marseille tracksuits I assumed it was them trying to cause trouble again. Despite glass everywhere I honestly didn't think much about it. I just thought 'twats' and carried on towards the fountain and the square. Even though I had had a few beers I certainly wasn't drunk, the other guys in our group had probably had twice the amount that I did. I was still in a world of my own as I turned the corner on to the square. I looked for Simples by the fountain and didn't see him so I called him again and asked him where he was now. He answered and said he was opposite the fountain by one of the bars which was pretty vague considering it was a square full of bars. I just said I'd find him in a minute and carried on walking down the square. Even though there were still thousands of England fans around I couldn't understand why there was hardly anyone at the bottom half of the square where I was walking. It seemed strange that there were England fans everywhere yet none at the bottom of the square where I was. I looked behind me and saw what seemed like hundreds of French police in their riot gear which looked like a cross between a Roman Soldier and Robo Cop! I didn't think anything of it so I turned back around and carried on walking towards the centre of the square where there were hundreds of England fans stood together facing

the police. The England fans were a few hundred feet away from the police and

were shouting a load of abuse at them. What I hadn't realised was that I had

walked into the middle of a standoff between the French police and the England

fans. It finally dawned on me what was actually happening when an England fan

took a run up and then threw a bottle like it was a javelin towards the police. Just

as the bottle was about to take flight there were about 20 England fans who

shouted in complete unison "no." I stood and watched the bottle soar through

the air completely off course and smash against a wall just above the heads of

two old French people who were stood there minding their own business.

Watching the bottle smash into pieces and being stood between the police and

the England fans it seemed the smartest move for me was to get away from

where I was and move to the safety of the side of the square. I wasn't hanging

around as I was expecting a charge from the French police at any second and

hedging my bets I'd say that some brave RoboCop was likely to slyly hit me with a

baton on their way past me just as a warm up for the soon to be free-for-all with

the England fans. Hot footing it to the left of the square meant that I was the

opposite side to where Simples was. I thought I'd stand by the side of the police who were watching the stand off from the side of the square. There were about 6-7 of them on the side standing in silence. I made sure I didn't stand in front of them, I really didn't trust those fuckers to just walk past me. My idea was to wait for the police to move the England fans on then walk over to Simples.

I did notice that a handful of other England fans were stood just behind me watching and mainly keeping well out of the way of the inevitable trouble that was about to transpire. What happened next genuinely shocked me and I can honestly say that I have never seen anything like it in my life. I looked to the left of me which was now the top end of the square which was jam-packed with England fans just having a good time in the sun with a few beers. Suddenly out of nowhere I saw these black figures running in amongst the England fans. The only way I can describe what it looked like was an earthquake or for Pompey fans imagine being in the Fratton End and watching the entire Milton End celebrate a last minute winner but with tables and chairs flying up in the air. For a split second I thought England fans were jumping around singing and having a good time. Then I watched in disbelief at everything being thrown around with people running in all directions, it looked really nasty. I stared at these black figures running into groups of England fans using metal bars, chairs and their fists to attack them. Even though I was a good few hundred feet away I could see they were attacking indiscriminately. Even England fans who were sat with their kids at the tables were being attacked from behind and without warning. It must have been between 5-6 seconds of the English being attacked before people started running for their lives down the square towards me. It looked like the scene from the god awful film Zulu Dawn where thousands of Zulus charge towards the heavily outnumbered British. With everyone running towards the opposite end of the square I realised that the hapless England fans were going to be running straight towards the soon to be oncoming French police. I'm not Rain Man but the French Police were not only complete cowards they were also totally incompetent. So I would have put my life on it that the French police would have seen the on rushing England supporters and assumed that despite having guns, shields, batons, gas and more armour than a Tiger tank they were being attacked by the unarmed English in their shorts and t-shirts and flip flops. I really was expecting to see batons flailing as the English got charged but it didn't happen. My view was blocked to the right of me because I was stood next to a police van. So the right hand side of the square where the fountain was I couldn't see anything at all.

Opposite to me was a lane which lead back to the port and a lot of England fans were running down there or were trying to run inside the bars on the side of the square to take cover. The problem was it caused a bottleneck which slowed a lot of people down almost to a standstill. I looked back to see if the earthquake of people was still going on but my eyes didn't get to the end of the square as I saw 10-15 men dressed in black who were running in groups and only a few feet apart from each other as they looked for England supporters to beat the life out of. From where I was at first glance and only being short distance away, they looked like ninjas. Then I realised they were wearing Balaclavas and scarves tied around their heads to hide their faces. I asked an England fan behind me "who the fuck are those, Algerians?" He said "no it's Russians." Russian hooligans hadn't entered my head before the tournament. Unemployed Algerians from the ghettos yes, but my mind was still focused on a terrorist attack while I was in France which was all I had been seeing and reading about in the media during the build up to the Euros. Some of the English were getting punched and being hit with metal bars, but were able to carry on running through the square or down the lane to relative safety. Police fired tear gas into the square. It was absolute carnage and this level of violence was not something I ever thought I'd experience going to football. Having a toe to toe with someone was one thing but this was something else. What made me feel sick was it was no different to one of those wildlife programmes where you get an antelope separated from the herd and it gets pounced on by half a dozen lions who rip it to shreds until there is nothing left. One fan who was a couple of hundred yards away from me was attacked by a group of Russians which was awful to witness. I thought to myself 'Where's the French police?' The ones from the far end weren't in sight. I looked to my left and saw horrified English faces stood staring motionless the same as me. I'd practically forgotten that I was stood next to France's supposedly finest. This is how gutless the French police were, they waited for the last Russian attacking the England fan to leave before they went over to help. A few of the police walked over to the England fan who was lying on the ground. One police officer knelt down and started to administer CPR to him at which point I really couldn't watch it any longer as it churned my stomach to see anyone go through that for no reason other than being an English football supporter. The French police from the bottom of the square finally made an appearance, and only made the rioting worse especially for the England fans as the police fired tear gas at the ones who had taken cover from the ferocious Russians. So now the English were getting tear gas fired into their faces and eyes, which meant that they had to start running from the cover that they had taken which anybody else would have done. The big problem though was that they then ended up running straight back into the Russians who then had a second chance of attacking the same England fans all over again. I could see the tear gas starting to spread out across the square like a thick fog and head in my direction. I thought that I was far enough away from it for it to reach me but I could see the tear gas heading towards me and the people around me. Everyone that was stood by me turned and made a quick dash for it up a road that was directly behind us and which took us away from the square.

Within a few seconds my face felt like it was on fire and my eyes were streaming. I was pretty sure that no Russians were in my area but just to be as safe as I could I sort of semi crouched between a skip and a car. I had another England fan next to me doing the same. I was about to get going up the rest of the road when the guy next to me said " I really need a piss!" I thought that's a good idea. So we both stood on the pavement going for a piss up against this skip with our eyes and faces still stinging when some Muslim woman sticks her head out of the bedroom window across the road and starts shouting at us for having a piss in the street! Obviously I wasn't in the best of moods and her shouting at us wound me up even more, so in French I shouted at her to "get lost!" Or words to that effect. She was really shocked, probably because an England fan could speak French and two men were going for a slash outside her house. She then disappeared in from the window, I just knew that she had gone to get someone. I was expecting her husband to come to the window see us and come storming down to us. No, not quite, the pissed off woman then comes back to the window with some little old lady, I'm guessing it was the mother who had come to the window. The old lady then started shouting at us out the window as well as the other woman. My face was still stinging and I thought it was time to get out of there as I could imagine all these different heads popping out of windows up and down the road. The problem was I had only been to the toilet once since I'd been out at the port and where it was so hot I hadn't needed to go again. Now I'm pissing for England and couldn't stop. The guy next to me who I'm pretty sure was northern was getting an earful from the old lady out the window. Instead of just ignoring her he moved away from the skip and loudly cheers as he starts waving his nob at her while pissing in a mid air circle. It was funny but I'd had enough and just wanted to get as far away from the square as quickly as possible. I started walking up the road and out onto a main road which took me away from the war zone of the port.

Once I was on the road I started walking in the opposite direction of the square, I didn't know where I was going but I could see quite a few pockets of people walking in one direction so I assumed that people were heading towards either the fan zone or the ground. The burning and stinging feelings from the tear gas had worn off thankfully, however my left knee was really starting to hurt. All of the walking and being stood up for hours on end had aggravated it so I was starting to slightly hobble. I realised that most of the people walking down the road were actually Russians who were on their way to the game. I stood out like a sore thumb limping down the road with my red England shirt on. When I looked again at the Russians walking along the road I could see that they were carrying flags and wearing football shirts. Seeing that they were all scarfers I knew that there would be next to no chance of trouble with them. I was more concerned with my knee and that I was starving hungry. Luckily I found a convenience store, probably the equivalent to a Co-op. I knew that it would be hours before I'd get to eat something else so I grabbed some vile baguette and a bottle of water as I was feeling really dehydrated as well as hungry.

I eventually got to the bottom of the road, it had taken a good 45 minutes to walk all the way from the port. I could see plenty of England fans sat outside bars having drinks and something to eat. I could tell that there hadn't been any trouble as everyone was relaxed and in a jovial mood.

Russian and England fans were walking in both directions so I took a punt and turned right and started walking to what I hoped was the right way to the ground. Despite the chaos and slaughter at the port with the Ultras attacking the English I was still determined to have a good time regardless. So I got out my George Cross flag which had Portsmouth FC and Play up Pompey on it for the world to see and started walking down another lengthy road.

I've always been proud to be a Pompey fan and to come from the city of Portsmouth. It's a working class city but it's a proud city and one steeped in history and being the home of the Royal Navy. Such great people like Charles Dickens, Isambard Kingdom Brunel, Peter Sellers and Christopher Hitchens to name but a few greats were born in Portsmouth. I'm proud of the history of Portsmouth, soldiers departing for the D-Day landings, HMS Victory, HMS Warrior, Mary Rose, The statue of Field Marshal Montgomery the hero of Al Alamein, opposite the D-Day Museum. Just some of the historical reasons to be proud to come from the city of Portsmouth. With the city being built on an island it does make it different from any other city that's on mainland Britain. Pompey fans are often lauded as the best fans in the land rightly or wrongly. But the one difference between Pompey fans and other sets of fans is that Pompey fans support the city first, then the team which is why there is such strong passion amongst the fans and people of Portsmouth. So for me any excuse to tell the world or literally fly the flag that I'm from Portsmouth I'll take it. I only had my flag out for a minute or two before a Bolton fan in his northern monotone started murdering "Play up Pompey" in my direction. I started chatting to him, my intro nearly was "Bolton, relegated, in debt and crap too. Being a Pompey fan I know all about that!" After a few minutes of chatting I actually asked him where I was headed. He said I was on my way to the fanzone and that the stadium was in the opposite direction. With my knee really playing up by now I had no interest in walking miles to a fanzone to watch Wales and get extorted whenever I wanted to buy a drink. So I turned around headed back the way I came and followed the crowd towards the ground.

As I crossed over the road I saw sat at a table with a beer each was Nick and Brad. I went over and asked them if they had gotten caught up in all the trouble. They had been caught up in the rioting but managed to escape unscathed. Tom was still AWOL and nobody knew where he was. I'd called Simples and he was with some other England fans and was about to get the train to the ground with them. I didn't fancy having another beer I still had fresh thoughts of England fans being attacked while they were sat at tables having a drink. I thought that if there was going to be more trouble it was likely to be outside before the game started, so I decided to head to my seat while it was still early. We all had tickets for different parts of the ground so I didn't need to hang around and wait for us to go in as a group. I was more than happy to get inside a near empty stadium that way I could take it all in and rest my knee which was throbbing and had swollen up.

Saturday Night Leaver

Getting to the ground was fine, but getting to the actual entrance meant that I had to walk in a big semi circle away from the ground in order to get back to the ground which was a pain in the arse. The area in which the Stade Velodrome was located didn't look the nicest of places, mind you so far I hadn't seen even one half decent place in Marseille! I found where I was supposed to be going, there were hundreds of police and security. I thought that they actually meant business with the security which gave me a bit more confidence in the French authorities. I queued up and waited to be searched. When it came to my turn I stepped forward and held my arms out to the side expecting a thorough search. I'm not sure if you can call patting the sides of the tops of my legs as a search but the was as thorough as it got. Then the security guard waved me through. That was the level of the French tight security! France had promised fans from across Europe that security was going to be watertight and that they were prepared for any potential terrorist attacks and for fans to remain vigilant but enjoy themselves. As I strolled over to a programme seller to get my Euro 2016 programme I did think to myself that if that was the level of security they had in place then anyone especially terrorists could get anything they wanted to into the ground with absolute ease. The French security hadn't instilled me with much faith in their capabilities at any point so far.

Looking up at the outside of the Stade Velodrome it did look really impressive. The way the stadium had been modernised recently with roofs being added and was amazing and just looking at it from the outside I couldn't wait to finally get inside it and find my seat. As I walked up the steps and into the stand that I would be sat in it was a great feeling to be inside and close to watching my first proper England game. It's easily one of the best stadiums I've ever been to, and certainly the most modern one. Last season I had the enjoyment of watching Pompey play at teams like Dagenham, Crawley, Yeovil, Stevenage and AFC Wimbledon, all with pretty awful grounds and tiny capacities. So England at the Stade Velodrome made a welcome change from being at away games where at times last season Pompey had more travelling fans than the home set of fans did for their own fixture. The ground was practically empty when I got to my seat, but I didn't mind, this was my first and probably last England game at European Championship. I wanted to make the most of it. I saw a couple of Leicester fans in front of me and asked them if one of them would take a picture of me with my Pompey flag.

I thanked the guy who took the picture and congratulated him on Leicester winning the league. It didn't take long for the ground to start filling up. I was in the end which was just England fans and as I watched people arriving and finding their seats I struggled to see any Russians. Even at a quarter full the ground looked like an England home game. As it got closer to kick off the ground was practically full and the atmosphere from the England fans was brilliant. It was a party atmosphere and everyone was enjoying themselves once again. I was back to having a good time at the Euros as well. As the two teams came out onto the pitch the England fans were in full voice, God save the Queen never sounded better or louder. It was great when the game started and England were looking good and totally dominating the match.

I'm really not interested in the Premier league or the Champions League. I find it very plastic and manufactured. Even when Pompey were riding high in the top flight a few years back with players that fans could previously have only dreamed of wearing the royal blue of Portsmouth I wasn't that fussed on the Premier league. After a few seasons I had lost interest in the Premier league and so did a lot of other Pompey fans. It had become predictable, boring, extortionately expensive and the novelty was rapidly wearing off. So when

Pompey's fall from grace was complete and the club was starting at the bottom all over again, it became exciting once more.

I have to say that watching Wayne Rooney in the flesh was fantastic. He was brilliant and you could see what class he really is and why he's been so good for so long. England were playing well and were fast pushing forward and whenever they lost the ball they seemed to win it straight back. Russia on the other hand seemed very pedestrian and unimaginative without ever threatening the England goal. I was confident England were going to score before half time, but it never materialised as England missed several good chances to be out of sight. As the second half got under way the England fans were giving the team excellent backing and England still looked the better team and the most likely to score. Despite Russia still being as bad as the first half time was starting to run out and England fans were beginning to lose patience with the side. They had already run out of patience with Raheem Sterling, he really was garbage and every time he got the ball in a dangerous area he'd slow the play up, cut inside and lose it. Sterling was getting booed and was taking lots of stick off of the England fans.Then with 17 minutes to go England got a free kick on the edge of the Russian penalty area. I was to the left of the goal, and had a perfect view. When

Dier took the free kick I knew that was on it's way in as soon as the ball left his foot. The ball crashed against the back of the net sending England fans into raptures. The singing went up another notch as England fans could see that England were coasting to three valuable points and opening game victory. It seemed an odd decision that at only 1-0 Hodgson decided to take off Rooney who had easily England's best player. The game still wasn't won but I did think that we would cruise home with a comfortable if narrow victory.

As the clock began to tick down it suddenly crossed my mind that from since I first started watching Pompey in the mid 1980's they have always been a side who regularly conceded late goals and throw away games in the dying seconds. Last season's defensive frailties late on in games ended up costing them promotion along with their inability to win games in which they had dominated throughout. I thought back to the play off final 2nd leg away at Plymouth where Pompey conceded the injury time goal that would inflict the fatal blow in a flawed season which would condemn Pompey to another season in the bottom tier of English football. I wrongly thought that England would show Pompey how to see a game out and collect a deserved three points. As the game went into injury time with Russia putting England under more and more pressure, it certainly wasn't the Alamo but England seemed to be having to hold on a bit more now. England were dropping deeper and deeper towards their own penalty area, and as that was happening I wondered when the last time was England conceded a stoppage time goal. I honestly couldn't remember, the best I could come up with was when Zinedine Zidane scored two injury time goals out of nowhere in Euro 2004 to beat a shell shocked England 2-1. That was the only time I could think of England throwing it away in the dying embers of a game. I stopped trying to recall whenever it might have been and refocused on the game as we were already well into time added on. At the very moment I went back to concentrating on the game the ball was crossed into England's penalty area and was met by a Russian head which looped over a static Joe Hart as he watched helplessly as the ball dropped into the net. The Russians fans erupted as their players mobbed the goal scorer Berezutski. It left England players and fans alike with their hands on their hips wondering how on earth England could have blown an almost certain victory against what was an extremely poor Russian side. I looked at the England fans around me, everyone was standing silent and stunned.

Within seconds of the equaliser two flares in the Russian end were set off. Then what sounded like an explosion was heard and for a few moments people around me, myself included wondered if it was actually a terrorist attack. The flares were still alight but hadn't moved which seemed odd as if they were there as some kind of signal. I stared at the flares trying to work out why they felt so menacing but I couldn't put my finger on it. The full time whistle was blown but nobody really paid much attention as the England players trundled over to the end I was at to give the England supporters the applause that they thoroughly deserved. At the opposite end of the stadium to where I was sat were the Russian fans on one side and England fans on the other side. I could see the England half of the stand was clearing in seconds where as the Russian half of the stand was practically still full. Everyone from the England half of the end seemed to be running towards the exits as fast as they could. I knew something wasn't right but couldn't see the reason why, then I saw Russian Ultras running into the England side of the end and attacking them. To the far right of the end England fans were literally diving over the side of the stand and landing several feet below on to the ground. I was expecting the French police to charge the Russians back as there was no doubt now that it was planned and the English were being attacked again and again were the victims of an unprovoked attack. Nope not a single police officer insight. There were plenty of volunteers around, not sure what they were supposed to be doing anyway but you can't expect untrained people who were working for free to dive in and take on Russian Ultras. The attacks on the English fans seemed to go on for a long time, again the attack from the Russian Ultras was down to the incompetence of the French police and UEFA who didn't think to segregate fans in what was classed as a high risk game. I could see English fans getting punched and kicked and no one was helping them. There was nothing anyone where I was could have done other than watch in such horror at the extreme level of violence against England fans who had only come to the stadium to watch a football match. It was then stood their along with every other England fan feeling helpless and angry that I thought to myself 'fuck this I'm on the next available flight back home.' Any interest I had in watching England or the Euros vanished there and then. It might have only been Saturday night but I had made my mind up I was leaving. My battery on my phone had died just before the kick off and I knew I'd have worried friends and family back in England who would have seen what was going on in the stadium and at the port as it was all over every news channel. I turned and joined the queue for the exits, everybody was quiet and sombre. Hardly anyone was talking, and certainly nobody around me could be heard talking about the match especially when you consider England had played well and had then had blown it in injury time. That moment and the game were instantly forgotten. I didn't even think about the game or the Russian goal, I really couldn't have cared less by now. As I left the ground the England fans from the stand I was in were all stood still. I didn't know why especially with the chance of Russian Ultras attacking being extremely high and seeing on the faces of everyone that they had also clearly had had enough and just wanted to get out of the ground and surrounding areas as quickly as possible. People were asking each other why everyone had stopped moving. Then we noticed that the only way out of our area was through one tiny exit. If the Russian hooligans did attack the English fans then people would have been crushed and trampled to death without a doubt as everyone would have tried to force their way out of the solitary exit. It could have easily been another Hillsborough and yet again more incompetence from the French and UEFA. Fortunately though everyone safely made their way through the exit and out into the massive carpark where both sets of fans were mixed together. There were a lot of genuine Russian supporters who looked uncomfortable and worried as if they were expecting a backlash from the England fans after what had just gone on inside the Stade Velodrome. I was walking past a

Russian camera crew who were interviewing a Russian fan when an England fan

run up and grabbed the Russian's scarf from around his head before running off

with the scarf in his hand. I wondered if there was going to be a few fights

between the rival fans as they were mixed together and tensions were high

especially from the England fans, but nothing happened. I think both sets of fans

just wanted to get away from the ground as quickly as possible. I had agreed to

meet up with Nick at the same place him and Brad were having a drink before the

game. It was dark now and in all honesty I couldn't even remember where we

were meant to meet them so I headed straight to the metro. I tried to get a ticket

from the counter and they only accepted cash. So I went to the ticket machine

and tried to get a ticket there but the stupid machine wouldn't accept my bank

card. There was no way I was going to walk back to the hotel from the Metro with

my knee which was absolutely killing me by now and had totally stiffened up. I

reached into my pockets in the hope that there was some change and as luck

would have it I found two Euros. I didn't hang about. I got my ticket and squeezed

on to a packed train. The carriage I was in was packed solid like sardines there

was no where to move to, I just had to stand where I was until people started getting off further down the line. I could tell that everyone on the train was relieved to be away from the ground and heading back to their hotels. I turned my head to the right and saw a man in his mid 40's stood next to me actually crying silently. When I looked at him I could see he had blood coming out of his nose and a deep cut on the bridge of his nose. The guy looked like a school teacher who would never have wanted to have had a fight with anyone in a million years. I guess it's not a deal breaker if you're a complete wanker and want to hit someone wearing glasses who is unlikely to be able to defend themselves. I felt bad for the guy, I was debating on asking him if he was ok, but I didn't think he would have been in the mood to be asked rhetorical questions so I just left it. I turned away and waited for the train to pull in to the urine soaked St Charles station. I limped the few hundred yards from the station back to the hotel.

All the lads were back and it seemed like everyone had heard a different rumour. We were hearing that the Russian Ultras had attacked the English fans at the fanzone leaving 7 critically injured in hospital. There was also some hearsay that a French woman had been pushed under a train at the station by a Russian and that a fan had been stabbed. The other rumour that seemed to be more substantiated was that a Pompey fan had taken a real hiding at the port earlier and was in a coma. That was a shock and was certainly a rumour that everyone

hoped wasn't true. Me and Simples had planned to go out for a few drinks after

the game, but everyone was drained and going out on the town after that hellish

day would have amounted to voluntary suicide. I said to the lads that I'd had

enough and was going to get a flight back to England asap. Nick and Tom had said

before they had left for the Euros that they were most likely to go back after the

Russia game. I jumped in the shower and my face and neck felt like they were on

fire. I almost fell out of the shower it hurt so much. I took a look in the mirror and

saw why my skin felt like it was burning, I'd gotten sun burned. With everything

that had gone on in the day, despite the hot weather I'd forgotten all about

getting burned. The annoying thing about it was that I had actually brought

suntan lotion with me. So after my shower that left me feeling like I desperately

need a skin graft I went straight to bed and put the day as far behind me as

quickly as possible. I got into bed and had a look on Facebook and YouTube to see

how much trouble there had actually been today. I laid there for about an hour

watching videos of the rioting and attacks from the Russians, it was sickening to

watch. I had a lot of messages from friends and family asking me if I was safe and

Ok. Everyone wanted me to return home straight away which was nice but I'd already made my mind up that I didn't intend staying in Marseille a minute longer than I had to. All in all the day was a complete nightmare and I was glad it was finally over.

Raging Bullshit

I woke up the following morning, grabbed my pad and checked my messages to see if I had any likes or messages on my Facebook posts from the previous day. I had a message from Mike on one of my posts saying that he had changed his mind about going to Russia for the World Cup. I replied back saying that I was busy that day too! I read the papers online to see what was going on in the world. My jaw dropped when I read the headlines that England fans were rioting with Russians in Marseille and again in the stadium. I started to read the stories and the columns by various journalists. I couldn't believe what I was reading, it was total bullshit. It made out that the England fans were out looking for trouble and were the reason for the rioting. Column after column of complete bollocks which consisted mainly of 'it was England and maybe some Russians, but it's England so where there's smoke there's England fans causing trouble.' I took a break from reading the news and went back on to Facebook. I was amazed just how many idiots who have no idea, don't watch football and weren't there where it happened can form an opinion and think it will be accurate. I think I did bite a bit and replied to some of their comments that they were talking shit and that I was actually there and witnessed it first hand. I got a few likes for my comments but no one challenged me on what I had put, that just proved to me that people will jump on the bandwagon to slag off something or someone when they have no idea what they are talking about. If they could have backed up their argument then they would have questioned my response. A lot of my friends on Facebook were messaging me or posting that it looked really bad and they could see it was the Russians who had started it.

The following morning me and the other lads headed towards the port to get some breakfast. Once we got to the port we went back to the restaurant we had eaten at the previous day, it seemed the easiest option. One of our group said it looked like there were Russians sat outside of the restaurant, but they were minding their own business and I think it turned out that they were actually England fans having a quiet drink. A couple of the lads tried to take the piss when I suggested we might be better off sat inside. I felt it would be less likely that any groups of marauding Russians were going to walk into a bar looking for England fans where as if we were sat outside in the open we would stand out like a sore thumb. So we sat inside and I ordered a pizza for breakfast. As soon as I had finished I said I was heading back to the hotel as I wanted to sort a flight out as soon as I could, so I called the waiter over and I asked for the bill. When the waiter returned with the bill I checked it and it said 90 Euros. He assumed that I was a really generous guy, he was very mistaken! As my order was different to everyone else's I asked for a separate bill. Some of the lads started winding me up telling me I was being generous which just confused the waiter. I had to tell him as best I could in French that they were what's known in English as "having a laugh!" After a couple of minutes I paid for the right bill and was on my way. The rest of the group stayed down the port as they wanted to spend the rest of the day on the beer, or as they say in Portsmouth "on the shant!"

Walking back to the hotel which was about a 20 minute walk and only needing to take two roads I decided to have a good look at Marseille in all it's glory. All I can say is if you want an idea of what Marseille is really like go on YouTube and watch Ross Kemp, Extreme World Marseille. Then you will have a pretty good idea of just how bad Marseille is. Walking to the port and back I had seen several homeless people each time I had made the journey. This time I decided to see just how many homeless people I could see. I found once I saw the first one I could see the next one. There really were homeless people every few hundred feet all the way back to the hotel. All of them were immigrants from North Africa and that included small children and families. Between the homeless were beggars that varied from small children, to old women. There were even young women with new born babies that were waving at people for sympathy trying to get them to give money. A couple of times I told them in French if you want money look for a job. I gave up trying to count how many there were is at seemed like half the residents of Marseille were homeless. I got to the steps of the train station and started walking up them. The station is on a hill so there are a lot of steep steps that you have to walk up in order to get to the top where the station and taxi ranks are. It was a hot day so the heat made the piss stained steps stink that much more. It was such a strong smell I had to hold my breath and run up the steps like Sylvester Stallone in Rocky! It didn't matter what time of day or night it was there were always multiple groups of homeless immigrants just sat around for hours on end, either on the steps of the station and bus stops or inside the station, obviously with nothing to do and no where to go. Marseille is without a shadow of a doubt the worst city I have ever been to. When I was part of the Portsmouth Field Gun Team I travelled to a township in South Africa and that seemed to be a nicer place than Marseille. I don't know much about French politics but Marseille has to be a city that France as a nation has written off as un saveable. Feeling tired and with my knee still aching and not helped with my

Rocky run up the stinking steps I thought to myself at least I can look for a flight

home then take it easy for the rest of the day. I'd already made my mind up that I

wasn't going back out again as I was sick of being in France. I still felt tired and

with there being a strong chance of a repeat of the previous day's trouble at the

port I didn't see the point of hanging around in the same place. As I got to the

entrance of my hotel there was a woman who must have been in her 40's but

could have passed for 60's was stood there and started talking to me in French. I

wasn't really paying attention to what she was saying, she said something about

her being hot. I kind of wondered why she was sharing this information with me

then it suddenly registered with me that she was actually a prostitute. It was

certainly a toss up between her either being a homeless person or a hooker or

maybe even a homeless hooker! It could have gone either way. She then smiled at

me revealing that her two top front teeth were missing. She looked like Pompey

Ryan in drag! For anyone who doesn't know who Pompey Ryan is, he is a Pompey

fan hence the name, with learning difficulties who travels on Westwood's minibus

a lot of the time and to be fair he does do quite a few away games. He isn't the

prettiest of people, he's got a head that resembles the surface of the moon and has never got the hang of using deodorant. I just looked at her blankly thinking to myself "is she really serious or what?" I then said to her "desole, je suis pede!" Which translated means sorry I'm gay! I then left the not so Pretty Woman and headed up to my room.

I started to look for flights but there didn't seem to be anything for Monday morning, the earliest seemed to be Wednesday which felt like an age away. My wife messaged me to say she was looking for flights and that there was one on Tuesday for £300. I said I'm not paying that much for a flight from Marseille to England. I had almost completely forgotten about the Euros and that there were three games a day on. I put on the TV only to find that some of the games were on a French cable channel which surprise, surprise our shitty hotel didn't subscribe to! I found a game to watch, grabbed my pad and checked Facebook.

I had so many messages either on my timeline or Messenger from people still asking if I was OK and if I had managed to get a flight booked yet. A lot of them were people from work and Pompey fans who I didn't even know. It really was considerate of so many people. One of the Pompey fans who messaged me regularly was Samantha Piggott a well known Pompey fan. She messaged me the previous day to check that me and the rest of our group were all safe. I replied

back to her saying that I'm looking to get a flight home straight away. She

messaged me asking if I needed her to pick me up from the airport. I thought that

was an amazingly kind gesture, but getting home from the airport once I had

landed was the easy part. Getting out of Marseille and France was becoming a

major problem. My wife messaged me to say she had found a flight through Easy

Jet leaving 10pm Monday night. I told her to book the flight straight away. Five

minutes later I'm receiving an email from Easy Jet to say that I have been booked

on the 10pm flight on Monday. That did feel like a great relief, as I hadn't enjoyed

hardly anything since I'd arrived. The only part of the trip I genuinely did enjoy

was the England party at the port before it turned into a battlefield. With the

pressure off I sat back down to watch the football, but was soon losing interest in

it. I've always struggled to sit through a full 90 minutes of a televised game unless

it was a Pompey game I couldn't get to. Even England games are a struggle, I will

virtually always skip any England friendly and even some qualifiers as they can be

tedious to sit through. One of my friends messaged me to ask if I had read what

Gary Lineker had said about the England fans rioting and shaming the nation

again in one of the papers. I hadn't done but I soon found and read the article that Lineker had done. When I read what he had said I was absolutely fuming. Lineker was talking complete bollocks. As a player Lineker was fantastic especially for England but as a person off the pitch I've always found him rather smug and pleased with himself. I did feel a little bit like those old American Vietnam veterans "you weren't there man" but I thought well he wasn't there and he's saying how England have shamed the nation once again. I'm no different to anyone else from Portsmouth, we say it how we see it. If I have something to say good or bad I'll say it to the person's face, it's unlikely I'd get a chance of a face to face debate with people like Lineker over England hooligans but I still wanted to say my bit even if it was pointless. So I went on to my Twitter account and tweeted Lineker. My tweet was @GaryLineker slagging off English fans when you weren't even there, you clueless twat. I was there when the Russians attacked England fans. I saw on my Facebook timeline a video of Russian fans attacking English fans. I decided to tweet it to Lineker. I messaged him again and tweeted @GaryLineker why don't you watch this before you decide to write a column of complete shit. You complete cunt. A bit later on I read that German and Ukraine fans were fighting each other. Still pissed off with the nob Lineker I tweeted him again this time with a picture of German and Ukraine fans throwing chairs. I tweeted @GaryLineker I guess this is down to the English fans as well? I bet you are one of those vote stay in wankers as well. I looked on my Facebook timeline and someone had post a hilarious reply to a Piers Morgan comment he made about England fans. @piersmorgan Is there anything more pathetic & embarrassing than our football hooligans? Someone replied, hacking a dead girls phone! I can't stand Piers Morgan, he's the sort of person you take an instant dislike to as it saves time. I thought 'ooh he's a cunt as well!' So I tweeted him @piersmorgan get your facts right b4 slagging off the English as hooligans. I was in the middle of that so know what happened you smarmy cunt. What incensed me the most is all these idiots in the media especially back in Britain were slagging off England fans as hooligans and it wasn't the case. All the England fans were on the same level, everyone just wanted to have a good time. If they were being idiots and starting trouble I would have soon cleared off as that's not my thing. Defending yourself is one thing going looking for trouble is something completely different. I genuinely did sit there and think what else will England fans would be blamed for next. Martin Samuel the well respected journalist did a piece on England fans which he said that even if England didn't start the trouble they were to blame. What he meant was that in the past England fans have caused trouble and would take over city centres, put up their flags and sing songs which some people didn't like. I thought he was writing complete bollocks and it was just a cheap shot at England fans who were the victims of Marseille Ultras, French police and Russian Ultras.

That was enough of being a keyboard warrior for one day. The messages I was getting now was from people back home asking if I knew about a Pompey fan who was seriously injured after being attacked by Russians. I said that I had heard something but not a lot so I went on line and sure enough there were stories of a Pompey fan called Andrew Bache also known as Pepe. When I read about what had happened to him and that he had life changing injuries and had to be put into an induced coma I felt sick and angry at the same time. I always think about their friends and family and what they must be going through. I didn't know him, I know that a lot of other Pompey fans did but it still feels like a family member that's been hurt because Pompey fans are very close knit and it really is like one big family. One of the best things about being a Pompey fan is that it really can fill a lot of voids in peoples lives. Nobody cares what anyone does for a job or what they have or haven't got. People can be having all sorts of problems in every day life, financial problems, relationships ending, but come Saturday, those problems are left at the door and they are surrounded with their 'Pompey family'. Another thing I love about Pompey fans is if you ever needed anything or were in some sort of trouble you would never have a shortage of people that would be there for you when you needed them the most. Reading about Pepe the Pompey fan and a Leicester fan who also ended up seriously injured in hospital because of the Russian Ultras did make me think back to the square where the Russians had attacked England fans without mercy. I realised that the England fan I saw attacked just in front of me was actually Pepe. I discovered it was him when I went online to read about the rioting at the port. I was shocked that it was him and that I had witnessed it. There were so many attacks going on against England fans I assumed it was someone else. Just because I now knew who it was and that he was a fellow Pompey fan didn't make me feel any worse than what I already did. I felt as sick as I possibly could be regardless of who it was being attacked or what team they supported. A person is a person and no one who comes to watch a football match should never have that inflicted on them. I thought of Pepe and what he was subjected to just a few hundred yards away. I asked myself was there anything I could of or should have done instead of standing and watching the whole thing. Even with hindsight being the wonderful thing that it is I don't think I could have done anything other than stand there. When things happen in life like some sort of disaster or terrorist attack people who witness such events usually say that the incident happened so fast. That was the case here, even though I knew straight away what was happening my brain was still trying to register it. I guess it's because when something like that happens it's out of the ordinary, it's not everyday life thankfully, people don't expect to see it. In all honesty If I had run to the aid of Pepe, the first thing I would have been running into would have been tear gas, and once you get that in your eyes and face it really does stop you in your tracks. Apart from covering your face and trying to get away from it you're not going to be doing anything else. Even if I had run into the group of Russians at best I might have been able to push one over as they were all facing away from me. I might have been able to get a punch in on one of them but that would have been it at best, before I took a kicking too. The bottom line was there were dozens of French police in both directions who stood and watched and did absolutely nothing at all. They saw the entire attack and could have stopped it within a second meaning that Pepe may well have had a few bruises and cuts instead of life changing injuries. I even looked at the French police that were stood next to me, they just looked on watching it. Everyone of them was dressed as riot police and were armed with everything needed to disperse the Russians. Yes the Russian Ultras are complete scum for doing such an awful thing, but the buck stops with the French Police they are the ones to blame as they could have stopped it but decided not to.

News was starting to appear in the media about who the Russian Ultras were. They apparently were ex forces, trained in martial arts and had to compete against each other back in Russia in order to be eligible to travel to France to attack the English. There were pictures of the Ultras with machetes and pictures of them all stood together in a field with no tops on acting tough. If anything it looked pretty gay! The Russians said that they wanted to fight the English as the English consider themselves the best of the football hooligans. I kind of wondered what year it actually was in Russia. Marseille in 1998 and Belgium in Euro 2000 and I'm struggling to think of anything noticeable from England hooligans since the 1980's. I think the Russian Ultras IQ's must be pretty low as they spent hours in the gym training and fighting each other, then they finally arrive in France and attack England fans with weapons who aren't hooligans and are just sat there having a drink and minding their own business. Beating up fans when they are armed and out number an unsuspecting unarmed fan isn't tough it's cowardly. They were also so brave that they had to cover their faces. They were either total cowards or totally dumb, probably both, as if they had done the slightest bit of research they would have known that 1500 of England's most notorious hooligans had to hand their passports in to the police so they were unable to travel to France even if they wanted to. There were rumours floating around Marseille that a lot of English hooligans back in Britain were gathering a small army to come out and exact revenge on the Russians. I was being told that firms from Leicester and Stoke were some of the ones who were heading to France. I know that some of Pompey's firm from yesteryear the 6:57 were there. I think it was more likely that it was in support of Pepe more than anything else. I'm sure these super tough Russians would have been aware of this, but apart from a little bit of trouble in Lille they soon vanished back to Russia. Surely if the knew that English hooligans were on their way to meet them and have a proper fight then they would have hung around? That way they had the chance they supposedly so desperately wanted which was to fight English hooligans. If they were still in France waiting for the arrival from the English hooligans that may or may not have been on their way I'd hazard a guess that they would have come out on social media to ask where the English were. But not a thing from them, which to me proves that they are like the French police,

gutless cowards who like to attack basically unarmed holiday makers.

The Bourne Identity Crisis

I started to pack my bag and get things ready for my departure out of this Marseille misery when I picked up my passport. I opened it up and out fell the main page of it. The really important page with your picture and details on it. It was due to expire in a couple of months time so was nearly 10 years old. I couldn't believe it as I watched this page drop to the floor. I think the words I said to describe my emotions at that particular moment were "you cunt!" I really did think at that point that nothing was going to go right all the while I was in Marseille. I picked up the page for the passport and placed it back in the passport and left it on my bed.

It was around 11pm when all the guys except Tom came back to the hotel room. Most of the lads were pretty hammered after a day of drinking down at the port. They had got separated from Tom who was still out. They tried calling him and messaging him but his phone was flat. His wife was trying to contact him and was getting concerned. The lads said that there had been even more trouble that night at the port with rioting. We were watching the events on Twitter which had Stan Collymore at the port doing some king of reporting. I really like Collymore and do think he is a great pundit with a lot of good views. I did love it when I listened to him hammer the garbage Villa players after their dismal relegation

from the Premier league a few weeks before. Fair play to Collymore he was in the

thick of it so he got to see that again it wasn't the English causing the trouble. For

his troubles he even manged to get tear gas in his face. After watching those

scenes I was glad I'd spent most of the day in the hotel. I went to my room to

move my bag and passport off of the bed when I noticed that the page that had

fallen out wasn't in the passport. I asked the guys if anyone had touched my

passport or if someone had taken it as a joke. Everyone said no, I frantically

looked around the room. I was looking in places where it was never going to be,

but I thought I might as well. The only time I had gone out in the day apart from

the morning was to try and find something to eat. I struggled to find anything to

eat let alone anything nice to eat. Almost everything I looked at was halal, and I'm

never going to eat anything halal as I think it's a barbaric way to kill an animal. I

wouldn't have been surprised if the fruit and veg was halal, I really couldn't find

anything half decent to eat. McDonalds look a better bet than most of the

brasseries and restaurants I could find, and eating a McDonalds at anytime is

always a last resort. So unless someone let themselves into the room just to take

my page out of my passport or someone took it as a joke which all of the guys said they definitely didn't do I'll have to put the missing passport page down as the Marseille Triangle!

Tom eventually returned back to the hotel and came in to our room where the rest of us were. Tom was covered in blood, he'd got into a fight with some Algerians down at the port. So two out of the three nights in Marseille Tom had been in two fights, both times with Algerian Marseille Ultras. Feeling annoyed about the passport I decided to go to bed as I knew I had a race against time to get a temporary one as my flight was departing at 10pm the next day.

I called the British embassy and spoke to a really helpful girl called Lisa. I started explaining about my passport page doing a disappearing act and that I had a flight booked for the same day. Then my signal went and I got cut off. I phoned straight back, this time I had some guy answer the phone and it sounded like he had a thick Nigerian accent. I couldn't understand a word he was saying. I took a deep breath and then tried to explain what had happened. I honestly think he was a cleaner or something who had heard the phone ringing and just answered it as he didn't have a clue what I was on about. I was actually pleased when my signal went again which meant I cut him off. I tried calling again, this time I got straight through to Lisa which was a big relief as she actually sounded like she knew what she was doing. She said that due to the trouble in Marseille a lot of people had needed temporary passports and that they may be fully booked up. She said to save time I could book an appointment online. So I looked up the British embassy and started filling the form out. When it got to booking the appointment the earliest was 10:30 am on Wednesday. I felt a burning feeling on the back of my neck, a bit like when you were a kid and you did something wrong and your mum's rumbled you, and knew it wasn't going to end well. This was 9am Monday morning and I knew that I didn't want to stay in Marseille a second longer than I had to. I asked if it would make a difference if I just turned up and waited at the embassy, the lady said she didn't know so I asked if it was possible for her to find out for me. Luckily Marseille had an embassy which was one big stroke of luck. I said that I'd be there as quick as I could. I asked for directions to the embassy and it sounded like it was near the port, so wouldn't be far to go. I asked Lisa if she would be dealing with me when I got there but she said no as I was actually phoning Spain. Spain! I thought I might have had a bit of fortune with

someone who was very helpful and going to be at the embassy when I got there. Instead now I was assuming I'd have to start all over again with someone else, hopefully not another Nigerian cleaner. I said thanks for all of her help and wrote

down the address that she had given me for the embassy. I asked her if she could

inform then that I'd be there in a few minutes. I thought that at least if I'm

hanging around sat there like an idiot tourist they were more likely to speed up

the process just to get shot of me. I put the embassy address in my Sat Nav on my

phone and set off to the embassy. I took headphones with me as I thought I might

need to call them if there was a problem like I couldn't find the place as I didn't

want to be wandering around Marseille with an I phone stuck to my ear. I

followed the Sat Nav directions to the port and turned left. I started going to a

different part of Marseille which I didn't mind as it said on my phone that the

location was only a few minutes away. I wasn't sure where I was going but it

seemed a slightly better area than the port and every other part of Marseille I had

been to. The route took about twenty five minutes and my knee was really aching.

Eventually the Sat Nav said that I had reached my destination. I saw a woman sat

at a desk through the window and thought 'well this must be it.' It didn't look like

an embassy, but I'd never been to one so what do I know? I went in and spoke to

the woman at the desk. I asked her in French if this was the British Embassy. She

looked at me with a very blank expression. I knew the Embassy was on the 2nd floor so I tried my luck and asked her if the Embassy was upstairs. Again I got no response from her. Finally she replied back to me in French that there was no embassy around here and that I was actually stood in a recruitment agency! I tried to salvage what little dignity I had and left as quickly as I could. When I got outside I checked the Sat Nav on my phone. The job agency was called the Atrium, the building that the British Embassy was housed in was a building called the Atrium. I'd put in half the address in my maps app and the stupid Sat Nav had assumed the rest of the address and sent me in the complete opposite direction. I tried not to be bothered about it but I was still really annoyed. I typed the full address in of the embassy and set the route. It told me that my destination was forty five minutes away by foot. My head was pounding and I was starving hungry and in desperate need of a coffee. I refocused and decided to head to the embassy on foot and when I saw a taxi I'd flag one down and jump in one for the rest of the journey. Of course with me having to hobble back from the wrong direction and a race against time I didn't see a single taxi anywhere. I could see I was going in the right direction as the buildings started looking very expensive and the area had a lot less beggars. My phone was ringing so I stuck my headphones in and answered it. It was another woman from the embassy in Spain calling to see where I was. I started describing buildings and landmarks that I could see. Suddenly I thought of the Jason Bourne films. I could see the similarities between me and Jason Bourne! I was limping around injured in a strange foreign city wearing headphones and giving out locations and landmarks similar to Bourne in the movies. The only problem was that I wasn't very good at giving descriptions or taking directions. The lady on the phone told me to head past a security guard and enter the building, so I did and when she asked me what I could see I gave her a list of shops. In the nicest possible way she had to tell me that I'd actually walked into a shopping centre across the road. I walked back over the road to the right building and at that moment the lady on the line from Spain pretty much gave up on me and probably life as well and hung up. About 30 seconds later I got another call this time from the embassy itself, an Irish lady who said they were expecting me. I told her I didn't know where I was going and could she give me directions. Unfortunately she was even more clueless than me when it came to giving out directions. Her directions sent me into the cleaner's cupboard and then into the security room where a security guard was watching CCTV just stared at me in surprise. I managed to finally find the lifts, but even then that wasn't straight forward. The lift numbers and ground levels are different in France to the UK which confused me and I ended up getting out on the same wrong floor three times in a row. So fourth time lucky with the lift and I manage to get off on then right one and found the door to the embassy. They let me in and searched me, I then walked over to the counter and fill a form out. I handed over my passport photos I had taken at the train station on the way to the embassy. The lady dealing with me said that I should come back in about ninety minutes as my passport would be ready then. I couldn't believe my luck. What a result that was. I'd pretty much accepted that I'd be staying at least another night in Marseille. She said that the embassy had prioritised me as I had a flight to catch. I was pretty jubilant. It even helped take the sting out of the 136 Euros I had to pay for the temporary passport.

I was in a building that had some designer stores and some fairly posh restaurants. So feeling pleased with myself I decided to get something decent to eat. I walked into a really nice restaurant that was practically empty as it was only about 11:30am. I ordered a really nice meal which the waitress recommended. Not sure what it was but it wasn't halal and it was the best meal I'd had since I landed in France. I sat there and relaxed as I was pleased that my nightmare was coming to an end finally. I stayed in there for close to an hour and half. I wasn't in a rush any longer, the weight had been lifted from my shoulders. My flight was at 10pm and even if the passport was going to take a bit longer I didn't care, I'd go for a drink and do some more relaxing. I looked at the time and knew my passport must be nearly read so I slowly strolled back to the lifts and somehow still managed to get out on the wrong floor again. Just as I got out of the lift the embassy called me to say that my passport was ready for me to collect. This was great, things were taking a turn for the better. I went into the embassy and sat down and waited. The lady dealing with me came to the counter and said she wouldn't be a moment. She returned a minute or two later, called me over and handed me my new lovely cream coloured temporary passport. I thanked her so much for doing it so quickly for me. She wished me a safe flight back to Britain. Just as I said thanks and turned away to leave the embassy I checked my phone and saw that a text message had just that second come through. It was from Easy Jet. It said 'We're very sorry due to air traffic control restrictions your flight has been cancelled.' I just thought to myself 'are you fucking kidding me?' I got outside feeling more than slightly stunned and headed for the metro. I was back in the hotel room in no time at all but was still well and truly shell shocked. I told the guys about the new passport and the flight being cancelled. Jay looked at the passport and said that the passport was dated to travel today and there was no way I was getting a flight out of Marseille today. I called the embassy in Spain straight away, luckily the guy I spoke to told me that it was valid until the 17th, so I had a few days in which to get out of Marseille.

Leaving Marseille was becoming more and more difficult. Tom and Nick were leaving in a few hours and their flight was fine. A lot of flights were being cancelled due to the French going on strike. The flights that were available were rapidly going up in price. Getting flights out of Marseille was difficult with the French strikes but there were also a lot of English who desperately wanted to leave Marseille as they were sick of being there and were worried about their safety. Simples, Brad and Jay needed to get a train to Lille to watch the England Wales game but the prices were really expensive. They were even looking for hire cars but that was far too expensive. I looked to get the ferry from Caen or Cherbourg straight back to Portsmouth but the rail fare was more expensive than getting a flight and would have taken ages to travel that far up the country. I called my wife and asked her to see if she could get me another flight. I said if you can just book it don't worry about the price. I didn't want to be in Marseille at all and I didn't care about paying over the odds to get out of there, whatever the price it would have been worth it. She messaged me a few minutes later to say she had booked me on a flight for the following morning. I had to stop off in Madrid and sit around the airport for four hours but I didn't care. The important thing was this time I was going to be on my way out of Marseille, finally. All I needed to do was get a train to the airport which was only a short distance and was about 8 Euros. Brad, Jay and Simples were still having a total nightmare getting out of Marseille. They had to check out of the hotel following morning and they had to be on a train out of there or they would be stranded in Marseille with all of their bags and no where to go. There was every chance they'd get robbed or attacked if they didn't get a train. The three of them decided to walk to the station and see what trains they could find. Feeling relived that I'd be on my way out of Marseille I decided to head to the port and have a pint. The Russians had gone and the port had turned back to normality. I found a quiet bar near to the square that two days previously had become an English bloodbath. The football was on TV and it was the Republic of Ireland versus Sweden. I've always been a massive fan of Zlatan Ibrahimović, so I knew I was going to have a decent evening in Marseille for once. I messaged Simples and told him where I was. The three of them met up with me a bit later on at the bar and we all had a few beers. The lads said they had managed to book tickets for the train to Lille and even though it cost them around 100 Euros each they were happy to finally have a train ticket to get out of Marseille with. I had a good conversation about the Euros with a couple of French fans which was great as I'm always interested in what other fans of different nations have to say about football in general. It also gave me a chance to have a conversation in French which I hadn't really been able to do since I had been in France. I'm definitely a 'when in Rome' kind of person, so wherever I am in the world I'll always try speaking the language. I didn't get much chance in Marseille which was more of a 'when in a foreign battlefield!' So I just wrote off the cultural side of France this time around and concentrated on getting as far away from Marseille as quickly as the striking French would allow me to.

It got to about 11:30pm, Brad had already gone back to the hotel, me Jay and Simples were happy to stay out and have a few more beers. As we got up and left the bar we had been at all evening, we noticed that the people that were about and indeed the mood had completely changed. It had gone from a lot of people having a nice time sat outside the various bars and brasseries around the port to pretty much just Arabs loitering around in groups. The three of us suddenly stood out looking like English tourists and there didn't seem to be any other England fans around. We weren't that particularly bothered we were just a bit more vigil as we headed along the port looking for another bar that was still open. Everything seemed to be closing for the night, then Jay noticed a bar that was still open. The entrance door was shut so we walked up to the window and looked through it. I could only see men sat at the bar having a drink, but something seemed a bit strange. I looked around and there was a group of French people looking at us which was slightly odd. I'd had enough by now and was done for the night. I said to the guys that I was going to head back to the hotel. They still wanted to go for a drink, so I thought that I'd walk back on my own. I stepped back into the road as Jay and Simples were still stood by the window looking in. I glanced up above the window from where I was stood and noticed a big rainbow sign above it. Simples and Jay were trying to get into a gay bar which made me laugh. It wasn't exactly the Blue Oyster club from Police Academy though, just a normal bar with a rainbow above it. I shouted over to Jay and Simples and said "lads you do know you're trying to get into a gay bar!" Jay turned around said he's been to gay bars before and always had a good time. I'm guessing that he must have meant that it was a pound a pint then! Both Jay and Simples decided to go in and have a couple of drinks, unfortunately for them they didn't get past the entrance as they were turned away for wearing shorts. So that was the end of the night for them and having any more beers. None of us had eaten anything for hours so we looked for something to eat which in the middle of the day was hard enough let alone close to midnight on a Monday. The only place we could see that was open was a McDonalds, so we accepted food wise that was about as good as it was going to get for us. We walked inside and the place was packed full of people wanting a midnight McDonalds. What was unusual was that it was nearly all teenagers and lots of small children running around. We are three lads from Portsmouth and Commercial Road is the city's town centre which isn't the greatest and it certainly does have it's sights. If you go to Commercial Road especially week days you're never going to struggle to find people that would be perfect for an appearance on Jeremy Kyle. But this did shock us seeing kids as young as two years old in a McDonalds at midnight running around. The queues were too long so we left and crossed the road to another McDonalds which was nearly empty and ordered something that resembled a burger. After finishing eating what could have passed for cardboard dipped in a ton of mayonnaise we started to make our way out of the port and back to the hotel. We were starting to get stared at by quite a lot the groups that were hanging around the port. We heard one Algerian shout at us and ask if we were English. We looked at him and ignored him and carried on walking. It wasn't too difficult for anyone to tell that we were English. As we started to walk up one of the main roads towards the hotel we looked behind us to see that a group of Algerians start to following us up the road. We carried on walking at the same pace. I said to Simples and Jay that if they catch up to us that we just should turn around and go steaming in to them. They both agreed that attack was the best form of defence, but when we looked back around a few more feet down the road they had stopped following us and had headed back to the port. We made our way past group after group of Arabs staring at us until we got back to the hotel. It was great to know that when I woke up the following morning and in the words of Simon and Garfunkel I really was going to be finally "homeward bound."

Planes, Trains and Endless Ordeals

As I woke up on my final day in Marseille it was a great feeling knowing that I was leaving. I checked the time and saw that I'd over slept and had to get to the train station as quick as humanly possible. My flight was for around 11:00 am and it was already gone 9am. I rushed around getting ready and went straight to the train station. I walked straight over to the desk and asked when the next train to the airport was and they told me it was 10:40. I mistakenly assumed that the airport being a short distance away and a fairly important location to travel to, that the trains would be pretty regular, I guess not! So feeling slight panic and breaking into a sweat I walked with a fair amount of pace to the taxi rank outside the station. I jumped into a taxi which was being driven by a little old French man. I asked him how much to the airport, he told me 60 Euros. I had know idea that over sleeping was going to be so expensive. Saying that I didn't really care about the taxi fare, the important thing was the taxi was going to be heading in the opposite direction to Marseille. As we set off despite being sat in the back of the taxi I could smell the taxi driver's body odor. It was so bad and so strong I could almost taste it. I had to open my window and stick my head out of it which made me look like one of those dogs you see going down the road hanging out of their owners car. He then started smoking which added to my misery as I don't smoke and the car became a combination of smoke and sweat. I was struggling for air let alone fresh air and holding my breath seemed the best option. Then Joe le taxi tried to start up a conversation with me in French. I wasn't remotely in the mood for a chat and having to do it all in French meant I had to put extra effort in. He asked why I was heading back to England and I said that I'd had enough and my holiday was a complete disaster, and Marseille was a shit hole. He asked me if I knew about the England fan who was seriously injured and in hospital. I said that I had and that it was awful and should not happen to anyone. The taxi driver did say that everyone in France had heard about it and were shocked and appalled at what had happened. I changed the subject and spoke to him in French about random bollocks until we got to the airport. After twenty minutes of pretty much holding my breath and making short bursts of conversation we arrived at the airport. It did feel great to know that one part of Marseille was finally behind me. I just needed to board a plane and see Marseille become a dot in the distance. I checked straight in and made my way to the departure lounge. I didn't seem to have to wait long until I was boarding the plane. Although I was going to have to wait four hours at Madrid airport I didn't care. Four hours sat at Madrid airport was not exactly a major problem after the last few days, I was just glad that the end was in sight.

As the plane left the runway tarmac and headed up into the clouds and on towards Spain I watched Marseille disappear into the distance. Most places abroad I've ever been to I would usually go back to visit again, South Africa and Marseille are two on the list of 'like fuck I would.' As I got off of the plane at Madrid airport I did feel like giving it some Braveheart and shouting out "Freedom!" I found what terminal I was meant to be at and headed to a Spanish airport restaurant to be extorted one last time. I stretched out sitting in there as long as I could giving me a chance to relax and have a break for a while. After spending a good hour sat in a virtually deserted restaurant I decided to make my way to the departure lounge. I still had three hours before my flight was due to leave but I was happy to sit there, wait and let the clock run itself down. When I arrived at the departure lounge it was completely empty which suited me as I wasn't in the mood for having a chat with anyone. I just started reading the news on my phone and checking Facebook to pass the time. I saw a message pop up on the lads' WhatsApp group. When I read the messages I was pretty shocked as Simples, Brad and Jay were having a terrible time in Marseille. They had got on to the train at Marseille to head up to Lille when they realised it was full of Russians. That wouldn't have particularly bothered them that it was full of Russians as they would have just found some seats together and minded their own business. The Russians seeing that they were English started threatening them and getting aggressive. For their own safety they had to get off the train otherwise they would have taken a hiding and with what had already gone on with the Russians and their level of violence they could have wound up dead. There wasn't anything else they could have done other than get off the train and having to write their train tickets off. The problem now was that they were without a hotel and stuck at the train station with nowhere to go or stay. There were no other trains running to Lille for the rest of the day and there were no hotels available in Marseille. They knew they had to get out of Marseille as being stranded with their bags with nowhere to go was extremely dangerous and asking for trouble. Back in England Tom and Nick were looking for hotels and ways to get the boys out of Marseille. I was so glad to be out of there but obviously I was concerned that they were in a really dangerous situation with no immediate way out of it. As the time ticked down to boarding I got a call from one of my friends and fellow Pompey

diehard Nick Popham. He had been following my status' on Facebook about my

holiday from hell. For some reason he seemed to think I might be interested in

going to the world cup in Russia in 2018. I told him to ask me in around two years

time as I wasn't really in the mood for watching England abroad at this precise

moment in time. As I was chatting away to Popham I noticed that my flight

seemed to have been delayed as it was due to leave 16:25 and it was already

16:55. I told Popham I had to go as people were starting to board. I waited my

turn in the queue to board then I handed my boarding pass to the stewardess. As

she took it from me she seemed to study it. After a few seconds she looked up

and said "I'm very sorry but this pass is for a different flight and that one has

already taken off." I was in total shock. I thought my legs were going to give way

like someone who had just been chinned by a heavyweight. I said to the

stewardess that the flight said it was for London. She said it was but my flight was

to the City of London airport and the one I had sat patiently for three hours at was

for Heathrow airport. I walked away in a daze, my legs feeling like jelly and went

straight to the customer service desk in a panicked desperation. I didn't really

know what to say when I got there. I guessed I'd just say "I'm really sorry but I'm an idiot who has just sat for several hours at the wrong departure lounge and has missed his flight, can you get me another flight please?" Or do I blame it on someone else? I couldn't think of anyone to blame so I quietly queued up and waited my turn to demolish what little dignity I still had left. I went up to the counter and explained to the lady who was sat behind it what had happened. She gave me plenty of news and none of it was any good. She said that most of the flights out of Madrid to the UK were being cancelled due to the French going on strike. Then proceeded to tell me that I'd most likely be on a flight first thing the following morning. Accepting that I wasn't going to get out of Madrid until the next morning I started dreaming of booking into a nice hotel, getting something to eat and having a decent night's sleep for once. The lady who was really nice and helpful said that she would make a few calls and see if there were either any spaces available or if I could be placed on a standby list. She made a call and spoke in Spanish, and guessing by her body language what she was being told it didn't look good. After hanging up she said that the flight she was trying to get me on was actually over booked and that even though they don't do standby lists I was still put on one. The lady did say that working at the airport all types of crazy things have happened and for me trying to squeeze onto a fully booked flight really wasn't that much of a big deal. The extremely helpful lady kindly made me a standby ticket and gave me directions to the right terminal. Even though it was a real long shot I was still eternally grateful for all of her help and thanked her for everything she had done. The kind hearted lady even let me off the penalty charge for missing my flight. I made a quick dash to the new terminal I had to go to which meant I would have to get a train out of the main terminal to a tiny satellite. I don't think I could have taken getting it wrong again and missing another flight. It felt like my Marseille misery was being strung out as long as possible. The flight I was on standby for was due to leave around 9pm, the time seemed to fly by. The passengers were starting to queue up to board the plane in no time at all which was a good thing to see, that way I'd know soon enough one way or another if I was getting on the flight or not. I wasn't going to wait until last to find out that I didn't have a seat on the plane so I pushed my way through the queue to the front and gave my standby ticket to the stewardess. She just smiled at me and said "here you go Mr Freeman" and handed me a boarding pass for the flight. To say I was surprised and relieved was an understatement, I couldn't believe I'd actually had a bit of luck go my way when I needed it most. I asked the stewardess to thank the lady at the customer service desk. I happily walked to the back of the queue I'd just pissed off in pushing past a few moments earlier and waited to board the plane. As I got on the plane I desperately needed the toilet, drinking all of those bottles of water at the airport had gone straight through me. I found my seat and walked to the back of the plane to the toilet. There was a steward who apologised to me that the flight had been delayed and didn't know when we were going to take off or arrive at Heathrow. I didn't know that we had been delayed and I certainly didn't care. Although I couldn't wait to get home it suddenly felt like I had all the time in the world. I told the steward that it was fine that the flight was delayed and said after the few days I have had this wasn't a problem at all. The steward seemed surprised that I wasn't complaining about the flight being delayed and asked me about what had happened to me. Before I knew it I was stood at the back of the plane in the department where they have all the food and drinks and I'm telling a group of stewardesses and a steward about my adventures in Marseille. They were asking all these questions and saying that they had seen the rioting on the news and that it had looked really terrible. After listening to my plight the steward very kindly gave me a mini bottle of red wine, which I thought was a really nice thing of him to do. After managing to work out how to open the toilet door I went back to my seat. I checked my phone and saw there were new updates from the lads trapped in Marseille. Because they were in such a bad situation and were unable to find either accommodation or a train out of there, for their own safety they decided the best thing to do was to get to the airport as soon as possible and stay there until the morning. Brad decided not to travel up to Lille and booked a flight out of Marseille for the following morning. The three of them slept the night on the floor of the airport. The flight back to England did pass by quickly and when we landed it was certainly a big sigh of relief. My sister who worked at Heathrow airport text me to tell me where I needed to get the bus from and what time my train was from Woking. It was a race against time as the bus was due to depart within a few minutes of me landing and making it to the bus stop was going to be a close call as there really was only a few minutes in it. As I only had hand luggage I was able to go through customs and then I was straight out of the airport and with the bus stop directly outside it gave me a few minutes to spare. The bus arrived right on time and I was on my way to Woking train station. As the bus pulled into Woking train station I got ready to make a run for it. I leapt off of the bus and just as I was preparing to sprint the few yards to the ticket machine I heard someone call my name out. I looked around and saw that it was my sister Stacey who was stood there frantically waving and calling me. She had recently moved to Woking and lived right next to the station and was going to get me a train ticket and give it to me in order to save me time queueing up to get one. It was such a close call because as I got my ticket the train literally arrived at the station. I thanked my sister for offering to get me a ticket and for giving me the bus and train times as I got on to the train and said goodbye. It was great to feel the train pull away from the station and know that finally my next stop was back to my beloved Portsmouth and home at last.

Back To The Sofa

Knowing that the train was rolling into Fratton train station it was a great feeling. As I stepped onto the platform at just gone midnight on Wednesday morning I took a picture of the Fratton sign hanging from the roof of the station and instantly posted it straight on Facebook. I wanted to let everyone know that I had finally made it back from France and that I had survived. I felt physically and mentally drained from the trip and a day of having to get taxis, trains and planes had left me running on empty. Usually I'd walk the 15 minute journey from the station to my house, but jumping in a cab after a day of travelling seemed the favourable choice. It was great to be back with the family and the comforts of my sofa. It was certainly a welcome feeling to wake up the following morning and get back to normality. I still had the rest of the week off of work and that meant doing the bare minimum and then spending the vast majority of the day on the sofa. It meant that I could relax and watch three games a day and finally see some of the Euros. In all honesty I'd lost most of the interest that I had in the Euros at the Stade Velodrome when I saw English fans running for their lives. You read and hear people say that when something awful happens in life then it puts football in to perspective and for me that was certainly the case with everything that went on in Marseille. When I thought back to a tournament that was still only a week old and that there had been people who had tragically died or had life changing injuries all through going to watch their respective countries play football I couldn't get past that, meaning that I had no motivation for watching the Euros with any real interest at all.

Simples and Jay finally made it to Lille and checked into the hotel that was booked long before the had Euros begun. By all accounts it was worse than the one in Marseille which would have taken a fair amount of beating. I knew there would be trouble in Lille as the clueless French Police and UEFA would again prove just how inept they were at organising and keeping supporters safe. The lack of foresight from UEFA in having fans of England, Wales and Russia all being in one city together with Lens only being a tiny place with a small stadium really is remarkable. Sure enough there was more violence with some of the Russian Ultras, but nothing on the scale of what went on in Marseille. There didn't seem to be anywhere near the same amount of Russian hooligans as there were in Marseille. Even though the trouble in Lille was far less than in Marseille I was still glad to be back in England. I watched the games on TV while writing this book and probably only looked up from my laptop when someone scored. Even when England floundered so badly and were humiliatingly dumped out of the competition by a well organised and spirited Iceland I wasn't particularly bothered. The manner of England's abysmal exit to the Euros seemed to be an apt metaphor for the entire trip, as in it started with so much promise and descended into a complete shambles. I spent the next couple of days replying to people who had messaged me asking if I was OK and asking me what actually did go on out in France while I was there. The level of fundraising and support for the seriously injured Pompey fan Pepe was truly amazing. His friends and Pompey fans had raised close to £30,000 for his fund which is an unbelievable achievement. Portsmouth being the working class city it is and with the cost of living these days made it even more remarkable. His friends had organised a football match to raise money and former Pompey players Alan Knight and Guy Butters turned out in the game with Alan Knight judging a best penalty competition. There was a fundraising night at the Que Ball club for Pepe which was a great success. It cost around £15,000 to be able to fly him back to the UK from France, which was made possible because of his friends, generous donations and some fantastic fundraising. Crispin Harwood who was doing absolutely anything and everything he could to raise money for Pepe even jumped out of a plane for the cause. That takes some guts to do something like that so you really have to applaud him for that. Pompey legend Alan McLoughlin kindly donated his Republic of Ireland shirt he wore against Malta which raised £700. That really was generous of Macca to do that, top player and a top guy as well. Pepe can now continue his long road to recovery with his family and friends close by. I'm just grateful that due to good fortune and circumstances I was able to make it back from France in one piece. I'm looking forward to the start of the new season and getting back to watching Pompey games from the Fratton end for the home ones and travelling up and down the country with the same old faces for the away ones.

Printed in Great Britain
by Amazon